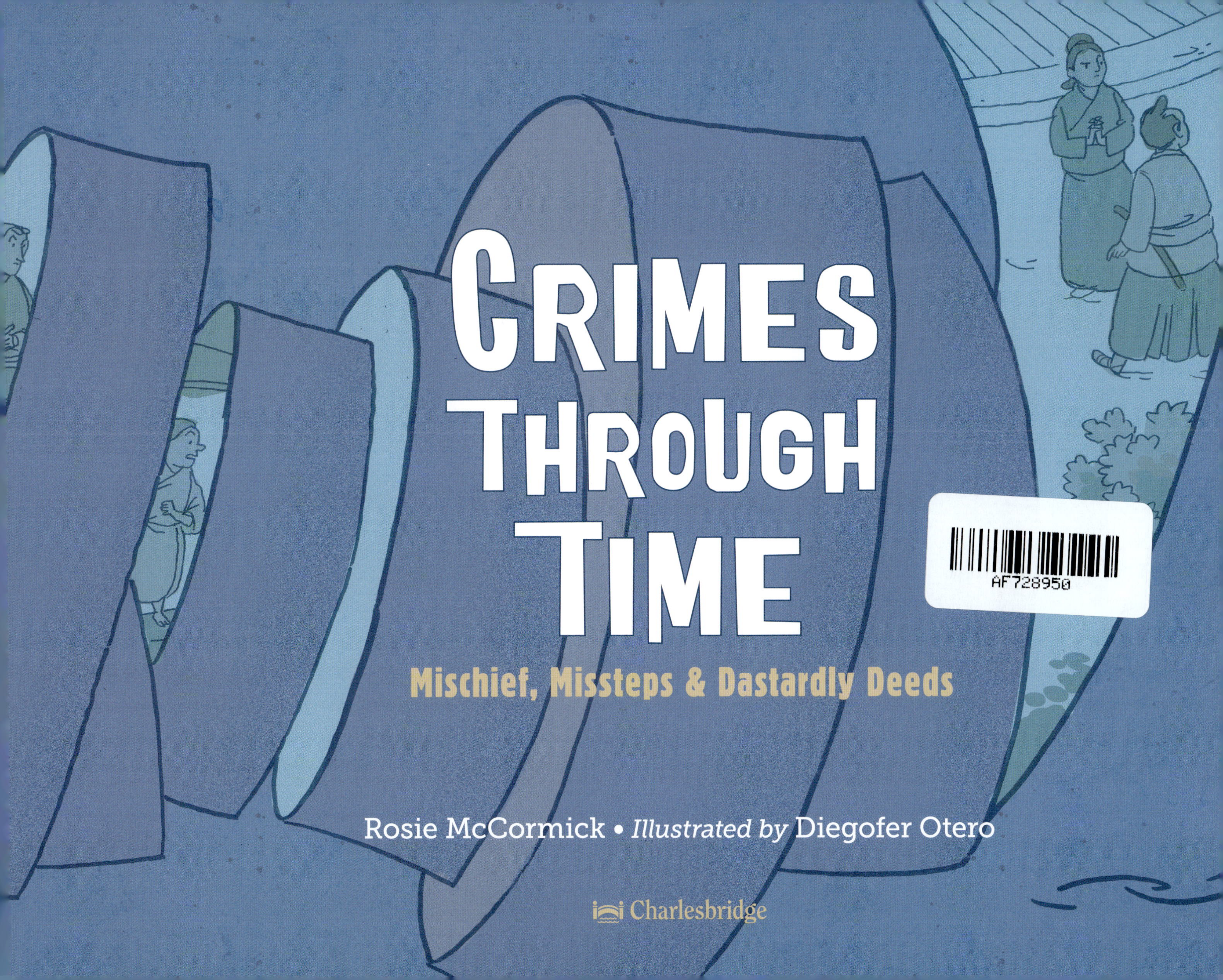

Crimes Through Time

Mischief, Missteps & Dastardly Deeds

Rosie McCormick • *Illustrated by* Diegofer Otero

Charlesbridge

Contents

The Challenge

The first thing you need to know about this book is that it comes with a warning. Criminals from different time periods and places lurk within its pages. For your part, you will be transported to eleven locations where crimes are underway. Anything from blood-curdling deeds to acts of desperation are possible, as are thoughtless missteps in relation to the law.

In essence, you will become a time-traveling sleuth. Your mission is to spot the criminals and their crimes. In so doing, you may just manage to stay out of trouble yourself!

This is easier said than done. You see, depending on the time and place, it might not be obvious what is or isn't a crime. Some things that appear to be crimes are not. Other seemingly harmless acts are forbidden. Perplexing, I know! But customs and expectations about law and order are homegrown. The one thing that *is* consistent is this: If caught, these criminals will be punished for their misdeeds.

Upon your arrival in each location, I will provide you with essential information. Pay close attention! Each briefing will include important facts about the place and time, as well as helpful clues about the crimes in progress.

Now for one final word if I may, dear friend: As you turn the pages of this book, you risk captivation, confusion, and repulsion—in no particular order and quite possibly all at the same time. I suggest you keep your eyes peeled, your sleuthing skills sharp, and your wits at the ready.

So off you go then to another time and place. I will meet you there!

The Author

I. *Crime Location:* Babylon, Ancient Mesopotamia, 1754 BCE

You have arrived in the city of Babylon, Mesopotamia, on a warm spring morning. It is the year 1754 BCE. The frantic squawking of chickens fills the air, almost drowning out the incantations of priests at the nearby temple. The priests are sacrificing the unfortunate chickens and offering them up to the god Marduk, protector of Babylon. Afterward they will examine the livers of the birds for signs forecasting future events.

Babylon will take some getting used to, but it is fitting that your travels begin here. The city is home to one of the earliest written codes of laws and punishments, thanks to King Hammurabi. There are 282 laws in all, and they have been recorded on a giant stone pillar for everyone to see. This is the land that coined the phrase "An eye for an eye," meaning that whatever is done to me shall be done to you too.

King Hammurabi's laws outline religious duties as well as day-to-day behavior. Citizens are expected to work hard, be honest, respect their elders, honor the gods, bury their dead correctly, and pay their taxes. Otherwise, they jeopardize the smooth running of the kingdom.

In addition to living by the laws of Hammurabi, Babylonians turn to their gods for day-to-day guidance. They seek omens that might indicate favorable or unfavorable outcomes. For example, should a tool, such as a plow, fail to function, the gods are warning of future problems. I strongly advise that you do not dispute such beliefs, lest you be forced to jump into a swiftly flowing river for blasphemy. Speaking of water, it is essential to life here in this desert land. So it is the law that canals, ditches, and all other waterways be kept clear.

As you make your way through this grand city, you will come upon all kinds of people. There are rich nobles, priests, and administrators who help the king govern, as well as police who help to enforce the laws. There are also merchants and artisans, and those who are enslaved. Know that there are dangers here too. Thieves, kidnappers, and murderers may lurk in the brightness of day as well as the darkness of night.

Your peculiar clothing may attract some attention. Nevertheless, try to blend in. Go with the flow, and like any good citizen, be willing to clear ditches, participate in religious ceremonies, and if necessary, drive a chariot into battle. And oh yes—make sure you try the roasted locusts. They are by all accounts superbly tasty!

I offer a few more pointers before departing: Do not argue, brawl, commit slander, aid an enslaved person attempting to escape, or give false evidence. If you wish to cast a spell, you must become a priest or a priestess first and then do your spellcasting in a temple. If you do become a priestess, do not drink alcohol in taverns. (But if you are a priest, that's perfectly fine.) Do not kidnap anyone, do not perform inadequate surgery, and make sure your construction skills are outstanding. Follow this advice and you should survive your time here.

Take care, dear friend. Stay alert as you attempt to discover what four things are amiss in the city of Babylon.

NOT GOOD.
MOVE IT!
SHE'S A PRIESTESS!
DISGRACEFUL!
SLUUURP!
HICCUP!

HALT!
THAT'S TOO MUCH!
WHAT'S THAT SMELL?
WAS IT A BAD OMEN?
WHOOOPS!
JUSTICE WAS SERVED!

Law & Order in Ancient Mesopotamia

King Hammurabi has established strict laws to help him govern his land. Law and order are important because the gods do not like chaos. They show their displeasure in many ways: war, famine, flooding, and drought.

Accusations of crime are first made in a court of law where at least one judge will listen to evidence and declare a verdict. If someone receives the death penalty, he or she will be put to death swiftly—often at the same place where the crime was committed. If accused of a crime such as slander, theft, dishonesty, spell-casting, or assault, the suspect may be forced to jump into the deep and swiftly flowing Euphrates River. If the suspect stays afloat and makes it back to the riverbank, they are clearly innocent. If the suspect drowns, that person is surely guilty, and the accuser gets to keep the criminal's home and property.

Nobles and others in positions of power are treated more harshly if they break the law. Priests are held to an especially high standard—understandable, as they communicate with the gods. But if someone accuses a holy person of a crime and *cannot* prove it, the brow of the accuser will be cut and marked.

If someone's teeth are knocked out, those of the culprit will be knocked out too. If someone breaks a person's bones, they will suffer the same punishment. Remember the "eye for an eye" rule.

What painful punishments await those who stepped out of line on this warm spring morning in ancient Mesopotamia?

Crimes & Punishments

Crime 1
Bad Building Work

Bad or careless building work is a crime under the law and must be punished. The builder, Adini, is responsible for the death of the homeowner's son. The penalty is that Adini's own son will now die.

Crime 2
Stealing from the Temple

It is a serious crime to steal from the temple. Dullupu is guilty of stealing a goat from this holy place. As Dullupu has no money, he may have to pay with his life.

Crime 3
A Priestess Drinks in a Tavern

Zila is a priestess of the temple. She may drink alcohol, but not in a tavern like a commoner. Now she will be put to death.

Crime 4
Surgery Gone Wrong

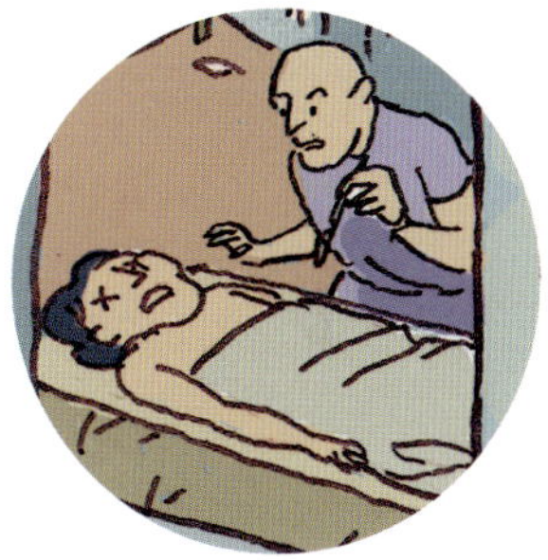

Surgeons are respected in ancient Mesopotamia, and the "eye for an eye" rule does not necessarily apply. This surgeon, Sargon, has been unlucky, or possibly careless. His patient, a nobleman, has died under his knife. Sargon will sadly lose a hand.

2. *Crime Location:* Thebes, Ancient Egypt, 1472 BCE

The west bank of the Nile is quite magnificent at twilight, wouldn't you agree? You are in Thebes, in ancient Egypt. It is the year 1472 BCE.

First things first: a warning of utmost urgency. The ruler, or pharaoh, of this great land is a woman, which is not at all typical. This extraordinary woman is named Hatshepsut. She wears a beard as a symbol of power and is served by nobles, priests, scribes, and a police force. Like all pharaohs, she is a god. You must *never* speak her name or plot against her. If you do, I will not be able to protect you from excruciating pain! Understood?

Good! It's also important to understand that here in Egypt the laws of the kingdom and religious beliefs are one and the same. The gods and goddesses expect harmony and balance here on earth, and crime upsets that balance. Those who create discord will be punished under the law. After they die they will be punished again by the gods and goddesses. So behaving badly is doubly unwise!

On the flip side, Egyptians believe that those who lead a good life will be rewarded in the afterlife, which is like life on earth, only better! In the afterlife there is no suffering. Indeed, Egyptians believe a person's soul continues on after death and can eat, drink, and live life to the fullest, experiencing endless happiness. Therefore, one's earthly body must be preserved because it will be needed again. And that is why these ancient Egyptians mummify their dead. Most mummified bodies are buried in the desert. However, the bodies of wealthy and influential Egyptians are placed

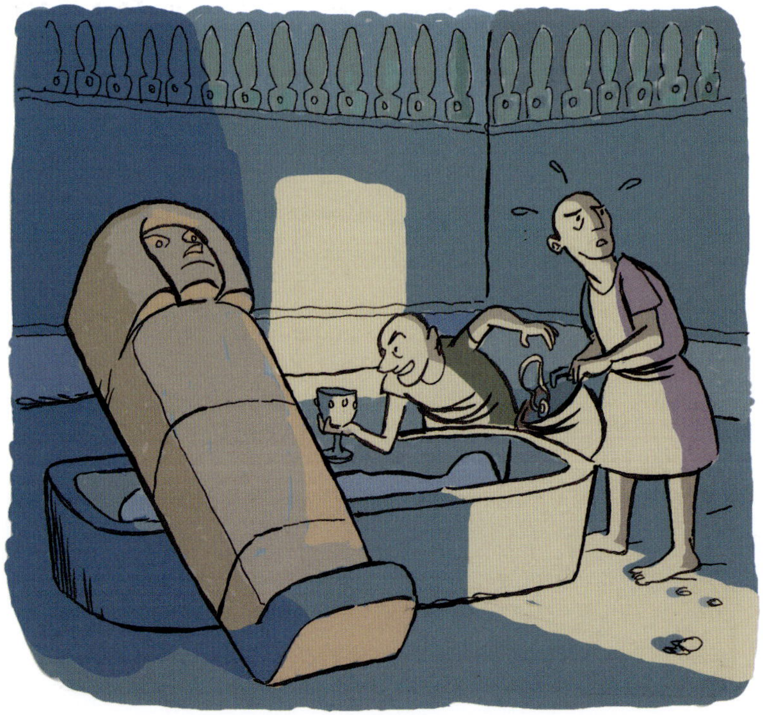

in tombs alongside their most valuable possessions, which they can continue to enjoy when they reach the other side.

This brings me to another warning: Tombs packed with valuable possessions are like jars filled with candy. They do attract attention. And even though some tombs are protected by trapdoors, deep pits, and dire warnings, tomb robbers are willing to risk life, limb, and the wrath of the gods to get their hands on hidden treasures. Robbing tombs is a grave offense, as is selling the stolen contents of those tombs!

Murder and theft are obvious crimes, but know that failing to pay taxes is a serious crime as well. For those in slavery, it is a crime to attempt to escape. Aiding a person trying to escape slavery is out of the question. You should also know that you can get into a whole heap of trouble for wasting water, eavesdropping, cheating, cursing, speaking badly of someone, or being a lazy oaf. Oh, and overeating and bragging are strongly discouraged.

Before you make your way through the busy streets, there is the matter of your hair to discuss! If you have any, you might want to shave it off. Being bald is preferable. As is a love of wigs, makeup, baboons, cats, curses, spells, potions, and board games.

Tread carefully, brave traveler, perhaps walking like an Egyptian as you attempt to detect the five crimes happening in Thebes this very moment!

YOUR TAXES ARE LATE AGAIN!
I WILL PAY!
DON'T FORGET THE DATES!
I WON!
THIS LOOKS VERY VALUABLE!
SHHHH!
DON'T COUNT YOUR CHICKENS!
CLUCK CLUCK CLUCK!
I COULD HAVE BEEN A SCRIBE!

OAF!
ZZZ
ZZ
THE PHARAOH MUST DIE!
BUT HOW?
THE BEST PRICE ANYWHERE!
OH MY!
HMM . . .
COME BACK HERE!

Law & Order in Ancient Egypt

Here in ancient Egypt, people believe that how a person lives their life, and whether they are virtuous and worthy, will be judged when they die. The goddess Ma'at is the keeper of ultimate justice. When someone dies, their heart is weighed against Ma'at's feather of truth and justice. If their heart is not as light as Ma'at's feather, then it is clear they did not live a good life on earth. They will not be admitted to the afterlife.

On earth the pharaoh and the chief judge, or vizier, are in charge of justice. Serious crimes go before the vizier—and occasionally even the pharaoh. During the court hearing, the vizier wears a pendant in the shape of Ma'at, or a feather representing Ma'at's feather of truth. For less serious crimes, important members of society sit in judgment.

A police force—with specially trained baboons—helps to maintain law and order. There are no prisons (or what you might think of as prisons), but there are deep pits where some criminals such as debtors are held.

Generally punishments are carried out swiftly. If a person steals something from someone's home, they must return the item and often pay a fine. Those caught stealing produce from the fields, or goods from the ports, might be banished; receive five cuts or one hundred lashes; or lose their ears, nose, or eyes. Enslaved people who attempt to escape can be shackled for hours or days. If they try to flee again, they will face harsher physical punishments, including beatings.

Because the wealth of Egypt depends upon the Nile River, people who disrupt the flow of river traffic may find themselves nose-less! The death penalty is given for the most serious crimes, such as tomb robbery and plotting against the pharaoh. The selling of stolen tomb items is harshly punished too.

What will happen to those who failed to follow the laws of ancient Thebes?

Crimes & Punishments

Crime 1
Selling the Stolen Contents of a Tomb

Robbing a tomb and selling the stolen items are serious offenses. By stealing items intended for the afterlife, the criminal is denying the dead person their just rewards. If Tabubu cannot pay one hundred times the value of the stolen goblet, she will die.

Crime 2
Unpaid Taxes

By law, everyone must pay taxes to fund the kingdom. The construction of temples and tombs must be paid for, and an army must be funded. For not paying his taxes, Sadiki will be taken to a public place and given one hundred lashes.

Crime 3
Lazing About

Laziness is not tolerated, as everyone must contribute to the well-being of the kingdom. Sarenpet will now lose a toe or a finger, after which he will be put to work.

Crime 4
Fleeing from Slavery

For trying to run away, Simi will be shackled to a wall for forty-eight hours. If she tries again, she will receive a harsher punishment.

Crime 5
The Great Crime

Nehi and Meri have committed the most serious crime of all: plotting the death of the pharaoh. They will be drowned, decapitated, or burned alive—the pharaoh will decide.

3. *Crime Location:* Athens, Ancient Greece, 584 BCE

You have arrived safely in Athens, Greece. It is 584 BCE. Athens is a splendid and powerful city-state with its own government and laws. It sits on rolling hills surrounded by olive groves and vineyards. The central market, known as the agora, is an important place where people buy and sell all manner of things. They also come here to discuss business, politics, astronomy, mathematics, religion, and philosophy. Athenians *love* to philosophize, and they are rather good at it!

It is fortunate you have arrived in Athens now and not forty years earlier. Back then a man named Draco had a great deal to say about law and order. He wrote a code of law that included infamously harsh punishments. He was *especially* fond of the punishment of death. Under Draco you could be executed for stealing an apple or a shoe. Things are a little different now, thanks to the lawmaker Solon. Much to the relief of the general population, he revised the laws and many of the punishments.

Solon organized the citizens of Athens into four classes based on wealth, giving the top three groups a say in government. This means the overall control of Athens is in the hands of wealthy men.

All citizens must publicly swear to follow the law. They are also expected to keep an eye on daily law and order, as there is no police force. But not all people here are citizens, or even free. In fact only free men over eighteen are considered to be citizens. Women, children, foreigners, and the enslaved are not.

During your time here, if you develop a strong liking for someone, you may throw an apple at the person. That is a customary declaration of interest.

Should you feel hungry, feel free to partake of the eels and the pigs' blood; they are popular foods. The skills of wrestling and spinning yarn are much admired—though not at the same time, you understand. Oh yes, there is the matter of nudity to address. You will almost certainly encounter people exercising minus their clothes—as in, stark naked. Pay no attention; this is perfectly normal, and for the record, not a crime!

As peaceful as Athens may appear, crimes are committed here. The most common crimes are theft, slander or gossip, unpaid debt, fraud, unpaid taxes, unemployment, dishonoring the gods, and being in the wrong place at the wrong time. Violent crimes happen too, so watch your step!

And now for some helpful tips: Do not be tempted to sacrifice an ox during a funeral. While we are on the subject of funerals, do pay attention to exactly *when* you visit the resting place of a departed friend—timing is everything. If you acquire a pet, keep it under control. Be particularly careful if you become involved in keeping bees, or selling certain fruits outside of Athens. Avoid people who speak ill of the dead. Girls, do not carry a basket more than a cubit in size, do not travel on foot at night, and do not be noisy at a funeral. Also, girls, do not be tempted to attend a public assembly.

Even in a seemingly peaceful place such as this, five laws are being ignored. What might they be?

TIME FOR A NAP!
GET A JOB!
A HORSE IS A HORSE, OF COURSE.
BUT WHY IS A HORSE A HORSE?
DIDN'T I SEE YOU SELLING FIGS OUTSIDE ATHENS?
WHO ME? NEVER!
I NEED A BETTER SPOT!
MY SISTER IS LOOKING FOR A HUSBAND.
ALEXANDER WAS A GOOD MAN.
BUT HE SMELLED LIKE A GOAT!
GASP!

SO NO ONE WANTS MY BREAD?
OWWW!
WHY NOT TAKE TWO?
YOU MOVED YOUR HIVES TOO CLOSE TO MINE!
BZZZZ!
BUT MY BEES ARE HAPPIER NOW!

Law & Order in Ancient Greece

Athenians do like laws. Laws control family life, religion, farming, and trade. Fortunately, Solon has found other ways of punishing criminals besides killing them. One of Solon's most popular reforms has to do with debt. Previously, if a person could not repay a loan, the debtor and his family could be enslaved. Solon has forgiven outstanding loans and freed those enslaved under Draco's law. Now debtors will not be enslaved, though they must still pay back what is owed.

When crimes are committed, the accused and the accuser have the right to be heard in a court of law. A council of hundreds of paid male jurors, all citizens over the age of thirty, hear cases. They listen to the accused and the accuser, who each speak on their own behalf. However, women are rarely allowed to speak in court. Instead, a male family member speaks for them.

Those presenting evidence are timed with a water clock. After listening to evidence and without discussion, jurors vote by placing discs into one of two jars—one jar for guilty, one jar for not guilty. If a person is convicted, the jurors vote on what the punishment should be. Their decision is final.

Punishments depend on the nature of the crime, when it was committed, and who committed it. As women and enslaved people have few legal rights, their treatment under the law is unequal, whether they are victims or criminals.

The most common forms of punishment are being banished, fined, disenfranchised, placed in the stocks, or forced to return stolen property. Often criminals are required to make offerings to the gods or make a public apology. Punishments for the most serious crimes include death by stoning, poisoning, beheading, or being flung from a mountaintop.

What punishments await the criminals who dwell in this fine city?

Crimes & Punishments

Crime 1
Selling Figs Outside Athens

To protect food supplies, it is a crime to sell food outside Athens, except for olive oil. Zoe will be fined half her fig harvest.

Crime 2
Speaking Badly of the Dead

It is forbidden to speak disrespectfully about someone who has died. Bion must make a public apology and pay fines to the family of the deceased and to the public treasury.

Crime 3
Being Unemployed

According to the law, it is a crime to be unemployed. Timo will be banished from Athens, lose his citizenship, or be forced to work.

Crime 4
Not Controlling One's Dog

Doris's dog bit someone's ankle. Now a three-cubit-long wooden collar, or restraint, will be attached to the dog for a period of time decided by the jurors. Doris will also pay a fine.

Crime 5
Beehive Sabotage

Markus has moved his beehives too close to his neighbor Ione's hives. It is a crime for one person's beehives to threaten the productivity of another's hives. There are also laws about the minimum distance between competing hives. As Markus has failed to follow the law, he will be forced to give Ione half the honey produced by his bees.

4. Crime Location: City of Rome, Ancient Rome, 44 BCE

Here in ancient Rome there is a chill in the air. It is twilight in early March; in fact the Ides of March will soon be upon us. You are standing in a Roman forum, or square. The year is 44 BCE.

It is a time of secrecy and deception. Julius Caesar is the supreme ruler of Rome and its territories. He is both consul and dictator—and an extraordinary military leader. Caesar has many enemies. Some members of the Senate fear he is now too powerful. You will no doubt hear mutterings about him as you make your way through the city.

Should you wish to freshen up before exploring, I suggest you visit a bathhouse, where you will be oiled and scraped before you bathe. Be aware that going to the toilet is at times a communal experience. The public toilets are large rooms filled with toilets but lacking interior walls. In other words, you will not be alone! Should you be invited to converse while on the toilet, do so. Otherwise you will be considered rude. Also, while enthroned on the stone seat, you might be offered a sea sponge on a stick. I leave it to you to figure out what to do with it.

At night, under the cover of darkness, Rome can be dangerous. Take particular care in narrow streets and dark alleyways, as the usual suspects abound. Only the wealthy are protected by private bodyguards. Should you be injured, I have it on good authority that cobwebs will stem the blood—some of it, anyway.

Nighttime brings other unpleasantries. Do look up as well as down! You may need to dodge falling poop. Some Romans illegally empty their chamber pots under the cover of darkness.

There is a strict social structure here in Rome. Below Caesar are the patrician, the senatorial, and the equestrian upper classes. Most of the people you see around you are plebeians, or commoners. There are enslaved people here too.

You will be considered a foreigner and not a citizen. Dress accordingly! Clothes reveal status in this city. Patricians wear white tunics made of the most expensive cloth, and only they can wear red sandals. If you have such footwear, discard it immediately. And do not wear purple clothing. This color can be worn by only the most important citizens. Senators wear a tunic or toga with a purple stripe to show they are members of the government. The expensive purple dye is made from marine snails gathered by the thousands and boiled. Enslaved people cannot wear the togas worn by Roman citizens. Only barbarians wear pants—just saying!

Do not sell your children into slavery more than two times, and do not bury anyone who has been struck by lightning. Do not help an enslaved person to escape. Do not hold meetings at night. Do not speak, or even sing, words that disparage someone's character. You *can* sell your urine as long as you pay a tax on the transaction. People here use urine to wash clothes—and as mouthwash!

What six transgressions are being committed on this particular evening in ancient Rome?

WHO'S MAKING THAT RACKET?
SOLD!
AGAIN, FATHER?!
TRA LA LAAAH!
WASN'T HE STRUCK BY LIGHTNING?
BOO HOO! SNIFF!
ALAS, TODAY I BURY MY BROTHER!
IS THAT SO?

AS A MOUTHWASH, YOU SAY?
QUICKLY! IN HERE!
COME BACK, YOU!
WHAT DID THE BARBARIAN SAY TO THE LION?
GASP!
THE NOT-SO-HONORABLE FABIUS STOLE MY LAND!
MY FATHER DOES LIKE YOU!
LET US MEET AGAIN TONIGHT.

Law & Order in Ancient Rome

Romans believe that no one is above the law. That is why citizens must memorize the laws as laid forth in the Twelve Tables, which are displayed publicly. The Twelve Tables outline the social structure in ancient Rome, especially with regard to social status and justice. The punishment a person receives depends on their citizenship status, their social standing, and even what hour of the day the crime is committed. For example, ordinary Roman citizens who commit fraud or forgery may have to give up valuable property, or lose an eye or an ear. Even a death sentence is possible. High-ranking members of society who commit the same crimes can sometimes escape severe punishment if they are willing to be banished.

Romans worship twelve main gods and goddesses. Those who fail to honor these deities are put to death. There are laws about burial rituals and how to mourn the dead. The behavior of priests is also strictly governed. The priest of Jupiter, for instance, is not allowed to ride a horse, touch iron, or go outside without a cap.

There are courts of law in which a judge will sit and listen to charges. Witnesses can be called to court to speak for or against the accused.

Even though thousands of people live in the city, there is no police force as such. The main focus is on protecting the city itself, rather than the bulk of the population. A number of volunteer citizens do act as a night watch, and privately hired guards keep an eye on the streets where the wealthy live. There are soldiers stationed just outside the city too.

Speaking of soldiers, those who commit crimes will be dealt with by the leaders of the army. Should a soldier run away and be caught, he will be put to death—as will every tenth soldier in his legion.

What punishments await those who carried out crimes on this March evening in Rome?

Crimes & Punishments

Crime 1
Slander

Speaking badly about anyone, especially an important member of society, carries a heavy punishment. Rufus falsely claimed that Fabius stole his land, so he will lose his own property.

Crime 2
Meeting at Night

People who hold meetings at night are suspected of plotting against Rome. Crispus and Abian are patricians, so they will escape decapitation. Instead, they will be banished to their estates, where they can focus on growing grapes, not revolution.

Crime 3
Running Away from Slavery

Enslaved people are considered property in ancient Rome. As this is the first time Drusus tried to escape, he will be branded with the letters *FGV* for fugitivus (Latin for fugitive).

Crime 4
Aiding a Runaway

Octavia tried to help Drusus run away. She will have to send an enslaved member of her household to Drusus's household.

Crime 5
Burying a Lightning Victim

The god Jupiter is believed to be responsible for all lightning strikes. Burying someone killed by lightning denies Jupiter a human sacrifice. Vitus, who buried his brother, will himself be sacrificed.

Crime 6
Selling a Child into Slavery More Than Twice

Selling one's child into slavery three times is a crime. Cecilia will be permanently removed from her family, and her father will not receive any compensation.

5. Crime Location: Chang'an, Imperial China, 692 CE

You are now in the great city of Chang'an, in China. The year is 692 CE. This is a city bursting with people and activity. In such crowds you will most likely escape attention—but once again there is the matter of your hair. A topknot is all the rage for boys. Girls, be aware that wearing your hair down or in a braid indicates that you are unmarried. Wearing your hair up signifies you do indeed have a husband.

The current emperor of China is a woman! And as a woman in a position of power, she supports greater equality for women. Some people refer to her as Sage Mother, though her name is Empress Wu Zetian. There are many whispered stories about her bloodcurdling deeds, but I, for one, do not believe such tales. I *have* heard the empress rules with an iron fist.

Much thought has gone into law and order here. Officials, judges, and the police force are guided by the Tang Code, which outlines laws and punishments. Empress Wu Zetian rules supreme, though, and her word is final. In addition, the empress has ordered the installation of public boxes into which anonymous accusations of illegal behaviors can be placed. It is reported that she reads the accusations herself!

The Gold Bird Guards are the police force in this city. Should someone commit a crime, however, everyone is required by law to assist the victim and attempt to catch the criminal. Be ready to take up this challenge.

As you walk through the city, the many shops, vendors, and street entertainers will draw your attention. Stay alert! Do watch out for speeding horse-drawn carriages. If the Gold Bird Guards are about, reckless carriage drivers might find themselves on the receiving end of a lash or cane. But sometimes such speed is allowed due to a life-threatening emergency.

Chang'an is especially busy today, as tomorrow is Examination Day. Young men have traveled from far and wide to take an important test. If they pass, they will be allowed to work for the government. The candidates will be confined to tiny, cell-like rooms or a large, crowded room, usually for days, while they are tested on many subjects. Rumor has it that some die of a combination of stress and exhaustion! No doubt your test-taking experiences are equally challenging.

I cannot stress enough the importance of poetry here. Boys, be prepared to write your own poetry.

Greeting people with an original verse or two demonstrates your educated status. Girls, you are off the hook: You are not expected to be able to read or write, although you are free to pursue such skills should you be in a position to do so.

A few guidelines for all: Do not question the notion that mirrors will protect you against ghosts or that brooms contain spirits. Do not incite rebellion or refuse to pay taxes. Do not cut your toenails at night, nor use the clippings to cast a spell. In fact, do not practice sorcery at all or make poisons—unless, of course, you are a physician. When greeting someone, interlock your thumbs and move your clasped hands up and down. This is only polite.

When the sun sets, the sound of beating drums will alert you to the closing of the city gates. At that point seek shelter and be on your toes. Street gangs, pickpockets, kidnappers, and murderers become more confident under cover of darkness.

Go now into the bustling city to see which four criminals are breaking the law.

AAAA! ERRGGGHH!
SAGE MOTHER HAS TO GO!
AGREED!
HAVE YOU WRITTEN THAT POEM YET?
STOP, YOU CHICKEN THIEF!
YOU DON'T SAY!
UMM . . .

A MIRROR DOES NOT LIE.
INDEED!
I WON'T LET THEM SELL YOU!
OUT OF THE WAY! WE'RE LATE!
STAND BACK!
I REPORTED MY SUSPICION!

Law & Order in Imperial China

Empress Wu Zetian rules over a vast land. Helping her to govern and enforce the Tang Code are numerous nobles, government officials, judges, military leaders, and the police force. The code aims to match the punishment to the crime. Therefore, the seriousness of the crime directly determines the exact number of lashes received, body parts removed, or hours of public humiliation or jail time served. Criminals might also face hard labor, banishment, or death. The most serious offenses include crimes against the emperor or empress, crimes against one's family, the use of poison, treason, and rebellion.

High-ranking members of society who commit crimes can sometimes receive a harsher punishment than commoners. The very young and the very old are usually exempt from more severe punishments. There are strict codes outlining how women should conduct themselves at home and in public.

When commoners are tried in court, evidence can be presented for and against the accused. During a court hearing, the accused kneels before the judge as an act of reverence and respect.

For petty crimes, such as theft, brawling, and drunkenness, the most common punishment is being forced to wear a large wooden collar, often while standing in a public place. Alternatively, a judge can order the guilty party locked inside a small wooden cage. Public whippings or canings are common.

Those who are imprisoned for not paying taxes will not be released until they pay up. In jail, rich people and poor people are imprisoned separately. Food and clothing for all prisoners must be provided by family members.

How will those who failed to follow the laws of the land be punished?

Crimes & Punishments

Crime 1
Use of Poison

Chun has poisoned his neighbor. For now, Chun will be exiled to a place where he will spend his days in hard labor, breaking rocks. Should the neighbor die, Chun may very well be executed.

Crime 2
Reckless Driving

For driving his carriage at dangerous speeds, Zhang will receive one hundred strokes with a cane. This punishment will be carried out right then and there in the courtroom.

Crime 3
Plotting Against the Empress

Plotting against Empress Wu Zetian is considered one of the most serious crimes of all. Gan and Gao will lose their heads—literally!

Crime 4
Stealing

For stealing the chickens, Fen will be forced to grind grain for a local farmer for a period of seven days.

6. *Crime Location:* Timbuktu, Empire of Mali, 1324 CE

Have you ever ridden a camel or set your course by the stars? These skills are not *absolutely* essential in life, but they may prove useful here.

The sand swirling about you is a clue to your whereabouts. You are just outside the splendiferous city of Timbuktu, on the southern edge of the Sahara Desert in Africa. It is 1324 CE, and the great Mansa Musa, ruler of all he surveys, is on a pilgrimage to the holy city of Mecca. If you are interested in joining him, simply present yourself to one of his aides. You will hardly stand out amongst the thousands of people already accompanying him.

In addition to all the people, eighty camels laden with bags of gold are part of the caravan. The gold is being distributed along the way to those in need, demonstrating Mansa Musa's generosity and the richness of his empire. Mali controls the trade routes across the Sahara, and salt and gold traders have made this empire wealthy beyond all measure. Salt is as valuable as gold, don't you know!

Timbuktu is the dazzling center of trade, at the very heart of the empire. If you choose to explore the city, keep your eyes peeled for the great ruler himself. He often mingles with his subjects and gives them gifts.

Mansa Musa is a devout Muslim, and Islamic law prevails. Not everyone here follows the same religion as Mansa Musa, but everyone must obey the laws or face the consequences. Specially selected guards, sometimes armed with poison-tipped arrows, help to keep the peace.

Timbuktu is a center of learning and openness. Foreigners are welcome here, and Mansa Musa insists that all people, including the enslaved, be treated with respect. As with every society, there are certain expectations. Therefore, I offer you some guidance before you engage with the locals.

If you are interested in becoming a trader, you must be an honest one. Traders must pay taxes on all goods coming in and out of Mali. Gold nuggets belong to the king, but you can trade in gold dust.

Outside the city you can eat food found in a field, but you cannot carry anything away. In the countryside you will notice that all the cattle are enclosed. This is to protect the harvest. Do not leave any cattle gates open. Do not light a fire near fruit-bearing trees.

Some residents here in Timbuktu practice traditional West African religions, so you may come upon shamans or sorcerers communicating with spirits or casting spells. This is perfectly normal. However, the use of curses is a crime, so it is best you refrain.

If you are a girl, you may marry at twelve or thirteen, but your father must give your new family three cows. Boys, you must wait until you are twenty. Oh, and should war break out, you will be required to become a soldier.

For the most part the merchants and traders around you are honest. But do keep in mind that where there is great wealth, there is also crime. What four crimes are being carried out in this city of gold?

YOUR SCALE LIES!
I SHOULD HAVE JOINED THE CARAVAN!
WHAT HAVE YOU DONE?
HOW MANY WOULD YOU LIKE?

HMMM . . . DID I PACK EVERYTHING?
WE WILL BE GONE FOR MANY MOONS!
FAREWELL!
MOVE FASTER!
MAY HIS CROPS FAIL!

Law & Order in the Empire of Mali

Mansa Musa is the supreme ruler of Mali—and also a very clever man. It is his aim to keep as many people as possible happy and content. The extraordinary wealth of his kingdom helps him achieve this.

The empire is broken into provinces, each ruled by a handpicked governor. Within each province, every village or town has an elected mayor, who is usually a tribal chief. Mansa Musa has given authority and power to the provinces, and he shares his wealth with his subjects, especially the governors, mayors, and other administrators. An empire with prosperous subjects tends to be peaceful and stable. And as for potential enemies—well, Mansa Musa keeps them close at hand so he can keep an eye on them. A wise man indeed!

As Islamic law prevails throughout much of the kingdom, there is a clear code of conduct. For the most part, laws are followed and taxes are paid. But crimes do occur, of course.

Members of a community, along with guards if needed, are responsible for apprehending criminals. Community leaders within the provinces judge most local crimes. If high-ranking members of society break the law, then the governor of the province or Mansa Musa himself will intervene.

Although Islamic law is in place, provinces can vary punishments according to local customs. Many punishments are designed to correct the wrong that has taken place. Serious crimes come with serious punishments. Murderers are most often put to death, as are those who incite rebellion, though some might be banished from the kingdom. Theft or repeated failure to pay taxes can mean the loss of a limb.

How will those who engaged in unlawful acts be dealt with?

Crimes & Punishments

Crime 1
Mistreating an Enslaved Person

Salif has broken the law by treating an enslaved person with excessive cruelty. For his mistreatment, Salif will pay a certain amount of gold to the mosque. The gold will be used to help people in need.

Crime 2
Use of Curses

The use of bad magic, especially curses, is unlawful. Fortunately for Khady, she cast her spell outside the city walls. Khady must give an offering of goods or gold to the mosque. Had this happened inside the city walls, she may have been put to death.

Crime 3
Dishonest Trading

The merchant Moussa has fixed his scales to cheat his customers. This is a serious crime, as Timbuktu is considered to be a center of fair and honest trade. Moussa will be asked to choose between banishment or the loss of a hand.

Crime 4
Murder

The crime of murder is an extremely serious offense. For his crime Abu will be stoned to death.

7. CRIME LOCATION: CANTERBURY, ENGLAND, 1361 CE

You have arrived in the city of Canterbury, England, in the year 1361 CE. The awful smell that fills your nostrils is the city itself. It's best to cover your nose and mouth! You are in what historians will later call the European Middle Ages, or the medieval period. King Edward III sits upon the throne of England. He rules over a war-torn, disease-ridden country. And now the Black Death has returned, killing hundreds of thousands of people.

A word of caution before you venture off: Avoid the open drains that run down the center of the streets. Argh! Never mind—now you fit in. Everyone else stinks too. Should you examine a drain more closely—which I do *not* recommend—you will see that it is overflowing with a hearty soup of muck, mire, and animal droppings. The contents are foulest on market day—and today is market day!

Speaking of animal droppings, pigs and rats forage for food in the streets. Pigs are valuable creatures here. Even in the city, most ordinary families keep a pig, which they fatten before eating.

The growth of cities like Canterbury has brought about an increase in population, as well as an increase in crime. Many of the people here are hoping to make new lives for themselves, but others are down on their luck. The poor, foreigners, and people with leprosy tend to live on the outskirts of the city. Those with leprosy are forbidden from mixing with the masses.

In this age of kings, queens, popes, feudal lords, knights, and chivalry, there are systems in place to help the king govern. But there is no such thing as a police force. Should you find yourself in a difficult situation, you will have to rely upon a knight, a kindly neighbor, or a night watchman to come to your aid. If all else fails, RUN . . . FAST.

Of course, there are laws in England—many of them. There are a number of unusual rules you should be aware of. When dining, do not consume more than two courses. Do not wear fur unless you are of noble birth. Although everyone drinks alcohol, including children, do not be in a public place while intoxicated. Do not go to church while intoxicated. If you find a beached whale, it is the property of the king, as only a monarch can consume its meat and use its bones and oil. Boys are required to know how to use a longbow. Do not engage in fistfights or otherwise cause a public disturbance. Do not enter the Houses of Parliament while wearing a suit of armor. Do not offend your neighbors by calling them liars or thieves. Do not meddle in the dark arts. And above all else, respect and honor the king.

Now go carefully, treading on eggshells—quite literally! And remember, Canterbury, like any city in the Middle Ages, is particularly dangerous after dark. It is then that thieves and cutthroats emerge. I strongly advise that you listen for the curfew bell. The bell is a warning to all that it is time to seek the comfort and safety of their homes.

Five misdeeds are underway on this autumn day in Canterbury. What are they?

NOT AGAIN!
A PET RAT, YOU SAY!
ROTTEN THIEF!
FOUL LIAR!
FITS ON EITHER FOOT!

HELP A POOR SOUL STRUCK DOWN BY LEPROSY?
YOU CAN'T BEG HERE!
THE KING WILL DIE BEFORE THE FIRST SNOW!
THE SICKNESS HAS RETURNED!
GOOD DAY, MY LORD!
WHO WANTS TO ARM WRESTLE? HICCUP!
PERHAPS I COULD PAY LATER?
CALL OFF YOUR PIGS!
OINK!

Law & Order in Medieval England

Kings have great power in the Middle Ages. It is believed that they rule by divine right, appointed to their position by God. Kings demand respect and honor, but in truth bad kings are feared and loathed.

King Edward III happens to be a good king—as far as kings go at this time. In the thirty-four years he has been on the throne, he has strengthened England's army, laws, and government, despite war and disease. As king, he expects everyone in the kingdom to obey the laws of the land. His family members, nobles, and chief administrators help him govern. The powerful Catholic Church can also influence his actions.

For ordinary people, lesser crimes such as drunkenness and debt are dealt with by a magistrate in the city, or by a feudal lord in the countryside. A person accused of a serious crime such as murder or witchcraft will be brought before a judge in the King's Court. Of course, all high-ranking members of society are tried in the King's Court for any infraction—no mingling with the common folk for them! Church courts deal with crimes committed by members of the Church, as well as crimes committed against the Church itself.

Most jails are only holding cells and not meant to imprison people for long periods of time. Convicted criminals face swift justice. Flogging, mutilation, and torture are particularly popular punishments. Murder, theft, and treason are all crimes that carry the severest of punishments: death, death, and death. Children who commit crimes might escape harsh punishment for a first offense. After that, they too will face hair-raising consequences. Punishments for most offenses are harsh. How harsh?

Crimes & Punishments

Crime 1
Drunk & Disorderly Conduct

William caused a public disturbance while drunk, so he will be locked in wooden stocks in the public square for twenty-four hours. Townspeople will no doubt pelt him with rotten vegetables.

Crime 2
Stealing

The young pickpocket, Henry, works for a master thief. Because of his young age, he will be branded on the cheek or forehead instead of losing his right hand.

Crime 3
Public Disturbance & Slander

Alice and Sophie have disagreed loudly in public and accused each other of being dishonest. These are two separate crimes. Both women will publicly take back their accusations. Then each will be strapped to a wooden stool in the public square.

Crime 4
Begging in a Prohibited Area

Matthew, who has leprosy, has strayed from the outskirts of the city, where it is legal for him to beg. He will be returned to the outskirts and ordered to stay indoors for three days. If he sneaks out, he will be banished from Canterbury.

Crime 5
Treason & Witchcraft

Ann has predicted the death of the king. This is considered treason, and it sounds like witchcraft. Both crimes carry the sentence of death. Her right thumb and left toe will be tied together, and she will be thrown into a nearby river. If she doesn't drown, she will be burned alive.

8. *Crime Location:* Tenochtitlán, Aztec Empire, 1510 CE

Welcome to Tenochtitlán, the rich and splendid capital of the Aztec Empire in the year 1510 CE. Moctezuma II is the powerful emperor of this great land. By all accounts he is a wise and fair leader.

The very first thing you must do is remove your shoes. Your feet must be bare, unless you are a noble—and I suspect you are not! Do not worry about hygiene, for this city is cleaner than other places you have visited. Tenochtitlán is built upon an island in Lake Texcoco. People move throughout the city in canoes on canals. I trust you can maneuver a canoe should the need arise.

You have arrived just outside the walled temple complex at the heart of the city. Behind the Serpent Wall are many temples, including the Great Temple, which is the center of the Aztec world.

Within the temple complex, priests are leading ceremonies of human sacrifices to honor the gods and ensure that society flourishes. Pleasing the gods is an essential Aztec duty, and it is believed that human blood is the ultimate gift to the gods. As you are not a captive soldier from a rival city, you will not be one of the chosen sacrifices—well, not unless there is a shortage of offerings. In addition to communicating with the gods, priests make astrological predictions and read omens.

Not too far away is the emperor's magnificent royal palace. There is a strict social order here. Emperor Moctezuma II rules over everyone. Beneath him are the nobles, who hold the highest positions in the priesthood, and then government and military officials. Beneath them are the lower-level priests, warriors, merchants, artisans, and farmers—and beneath *them* are those who are enslaved.

You should be aware that there are laws governing the clothes worn by certain social classes. It is not permitted for a commoner such as yourself to wear a cotton cape, feathers, or gold. Nor can you wear fancy ear, lip, or nose plugs. Do partake of the popcorn and chocolate should you become hungry, though; the Aztecs are rather partial to these foods! That

said, chocolate, or cacao, might not taste *quite* like how you imagine. And to confuse you even more, cacao beans are also used as currency! If you like dancing, you've come to the right place. Young people are permitted to dance all night.

The Aztecs do not approve of extreme emotions or actions. They like *everything* in moderation, and they have many laws and codes of conduct. As you can imagine, theft, murder, and treason are serious crimes. Do not get drunk—though the elderly are excluded from this law. Do not imitate a noble, incite rebellion, lie in court under oath, practice dark magic, steal from a temple, or brawl. Do not slander, or lie about, others, especially the powerful and influential. Do not destroy crops, and do not light a fire in a wooded area without permission.

Harsh punishments for unlawful behavior do not deter those intent on breaking the law. At day's end, when you hear the conch shells blowing, seek shelter if you can. Go cautiously as always.

Which six people are not behaving as they should?

LA! LA! BURP!
YOUR MEDICINES ARE HARMFUL.
YUM!
HOW DARE YOU?
MAY I TASTE THAT?
SHOULD WE BUY SOME FISH?
WE MUST CELEBRATE THE BIRTH OF YOUR SON!
BRING THOSE BACK!

O TOCI, GODDESS OF HEALING, CAST UEMAN INTO DARKNESS!
YES, YOU MAY MARRY MY SISTER!
I'LL SHOW YOU!
YOU ARE NOT OLD ENOUGH TO BE A WARRIOR.

Law & Order in the Aztec Empire

Laws in the Aztec Empire focus on maintaining the social order and not harming the balance of society. Caring for and pleasing the gods helps to achieve this goal. A person's gender and place in society structure their lives, from the laws they follow to the homes they live in, the clothes they wear, the jobs they do, the taxes they pay, whom they marry, and whether or not they have military duties. Those at the top of the social order have more power, but they receive the harshest punishments when they break the law. Men and boys have more legal rights than women and girls.

Less serious crimes are dealt with in lower courts by judges who are also warriors. Those accused can speak in court in their own defense. They can also invite witnesses to speak on their behalf.

Serious crimes, such as murder and rebellion, are tried in a higher court by a higher-ranking judge—or occasionally by the emperor himself. Laws and punishments are recorded by scribes in the form of symbolic pictures, called pictograms, or memorized and sung out loud by specially chosen speakers with incredible memories.

Although prisoners are sometimes locked in wooden cages and put on public display, there are no prisons. Punishments for crimes tend to be immediate. There are a number of ways a person can be put to death, including being stoned, burned alive, or sacrificed. The punishment for theft depends on the value of the stolen item. Anyone who steals an item more valuable than twenty ears of corn faces death. Anything less than that value must be repaid with interest.

Fighting in public is forbidden. If someone is injured, the person who caused the injuries will pay for a doctor. Drinking alcohol is allowed only on certain occasions, such as the birth of a child, a wedding, or a religious holiday. However, this law does not apply to the elderly; they can consume alcohol freely.

Children under ten are forgiven if they disobey a law, but parents may punish them if they are constantly unruly at home. Disobedient children may be forced to breathe in the fumes of burning chili peppers!

What punishments await the perpetrators of crimes here in Tenochtitlán?

Crimes & Punishments

Crime 1
Brawling

Matlal and Zollin have been fighting, which upsets the order of daily life. They will both be pricked with sharp pine branches until blood is drawn.

Crime 2
Wearing Sandals & Being Drunk

Even though Nochtli is a commoner, he wore sandals in the city. He also got drunk in public. As these are his first offenses, Nochtli will escape the death penalty, but his head will be shaved and his home destroyed.

Crime 3
Slander

Tlacapan has falsely accused a healer of being dishonest. Slander is a very serious crime. Tlacapan's home will be demolished.

Crime 4
Stealing

Nenetl stole eggs from the market seller Yaotl. Fortunately for Nenetl, the value of the eggs is below the value of twenty ears of corn, so she will not die. If she cannot replace the eggs, her head will be shaved and she will be forced to work for Yaotl for several weeks.

Crime 5
Practicing Dark Magic

Tototl has cast a spell intended to harm the nobleman Ueman. Tototl is a priest, which makes his crime even worse. Now he will be stoned to death.

Crime 6
Stealing from a Temple

Stealing from a temple is an act against the gods, and therefore an act that could harm the balance of Aztec society. Patli will have his heart removed.

9. Crime Location: Edo, Japan, 1622 CE

You are now in the bustling and vibrant castle city of Edo, on the island of Honshu, in the country of Japan. It is 1622 CE. The powerful shogun Tokugawa Hidetada is the supreme military leader of Japan, and this is his home. The city itself is alive with merchants, artists, and entertainers. Pilgrims, too, make their way through the city to visit holy shrines or temples. An exciting new form of theater is growing in popularity here. It is called kabuki, and it combines dance, song, and storytelling.

It is the age of the samurai, and their power is evident everywhere. In case you didn't know, the samurai are an elite class of nobles who are specially trained in the art of warfare. It is their right to carry both a long and a short sword, so you should proceed with great caution. If a samurai thinks you are acting in an offensive or insulting manner, he may strike and even kill you with his sword. So keep your eyes peeled and your ears open. Breathe in. Breathe out. Be calm!

I must confess, this is perhaps *not* the best time for you to be in Japan. Most foreigners or outsiders are despised and, if found, killed. Because of this, you might consider wearing a kasa, or conical hat, to blend in. Girls, you might also blacken your teeth for a more fashionable look.

Law and order are of the utmost importance in Japan. There are laws that govern what you wear, what you eat, whom you talk to, where you live, what education you receive, which taxes you pay, and even what happens after you have used the bathroom. It's true! Night soil, or human poop, is collected and used to fertilize crops. Anyone caught stealing it is punished.

In addition to NOT stealing night soil, do not wear silk, gamble, or carry a long sword. If you find yourself eating noodles, slurp loudly—this is the polite thing to do. And speaking of food, it is illegal to sell or eat fugu, otherwise known as pufferfish. So as not to draw too much attention to yourself, do not blow your nose in public or serve yourself tea. These are not crimes but rather incredibly impolite actions! Avoid giving your surname, as commoners are not allowed to use last names. Do not publicly disagree with the laws of the land. Finally, if asked to assist with a building project, say yes. Follow these rules, and you should survive!

On that note, I suggest you go forth with vigilance. There are many people packed into this city, and who can truly know the intentions of some or the desperation of others? Listen for the ringing of the bells that will announce the setting of the sun.

Now, can you uncover the five crimes occurring in this feudal castle city?

I WIN AGAIN!
PSSST! WANT TO BUY SOME FISH?
THAT'S THE GUY!
DELIVER THIS MESSAGE RIGHT AWAY!
YOU ARE MISTAKEN!
YOU'LL GET USED TO THE SMELL.
PEE-YEW!

THE RICE WILL GROW—HICCUP!
EVEN IN THE SNOW—HICCUP!
AND FOR MY NEXT TRICK . . .
INCREDIBLE!
NO ONE WILL SUSPECT A THING!
NOW WHERE DID IT GO?
HEY! I KNOW YOU!

Law & Order in Feudal Japan

Although an emperor sits on the throne, his role is largely symbolic. The shogun is the true head of the government, and the samurai class and the feudal lords report directly to him. Samurai warriors follow a strict behavioral code known as bushido. In special cases girls can become samurai.

The city of Edo has two magistrates, who are also trained samurai. The magistrates do not serve together. One serves for a month, and then the other takes over. The shogun does not want to dilute his power, so he will not allow any one person to have too much authority.

Generally, when a crime takes place, one of the magistrates and his staff investigate the matter, gathering evidence and speaking to witnesses. During this time the accused is held in jail. After the investigation, a verdict will be announced. If the accused is found guilty, they will be punished. But if there is not enough evidence, they will be released.

When there are multiple suspects and a lack of evidence, community leaders sometimes invite people to vote for the most likely culprit. The person who receives the highest number of votes is declared guilty.

In Edo it is difficult to get away with a crime. The neighborhood watch is vigilant. Most townspeople will also eagerly attempt to stop a criminal.

The most common punishments are fines, caning, whipping, ostracism, banishment, the loss of a body part, hard labor, and the death penalty. You could also have your crimes tattooed on your body. From time to time a criminal's family or entire village may also be punished—but that depends upon the seriousness of the crime.

What fate awaits the criminals who broke the law?

Crimes & Punishments

Crime 1
Stealing Night Soil

Selling night soil to farmers as fertilizer is a profitable business. This is not the first time Mimi and Jiro have been caught stealing night soil from a merchant. Now they will have their arms tattooed.

Crime 2
Setting Fire to a Building

Arson is an extremely serious crime in this city of close-packed wooden buildings. Shinjo's punishment will be swift and deadly. He will be burned at the stake.

Crime 3
Selling Fugu

Poisonous fugu will kill a person within hours if not carefully prepared. For illegally selling this fish, Aiko will be hanged.

Crime 4
Gambling

Gambling is illegal. This is the first time either Torakichi or Seikichi has been caught gambling, so they will be released after a flogging.

Crime 5
Drunkenness & Disrespecting a Samurai

Taro had too much to drink *and* failed to respectfully bow to a samurai. The second crime is the more serious of the two. The samurai now has the right to maim Taro or even take his life.

10. Crime Location: Williamsburg, Virginia, 1765 CE

Well now! Here you are on Duke of Gloucester Street, in Williamsburg, Virginia. It is 1765 CE, and Virginia is one of the most populous of the thirteen British colonies. This street is the main thoroughfare in Williamsburg. As you stroll about, you will undoubtedly encounter many of the ladies and gentlemen of this town. Consider offering up the occasional polite bow or curtsy. Do not stare at the British soldiers marching by. They are a common sight, as they are quartered, or housed, by the townsfolk.

You will no doubt notice that some people here drink copious amounts of tea. If invited to partake, my advice is to drink up. Many townsfolk carry smelling salts to sniff when they are feeling faint—and most everyone knows how to dance the minuet. If you do not, perhaps you would like to learn—it *is* all the rage!

This is an interesting time to be in the colonies. Angry colonists have challenged the laws of King George III. The Stamp Act is the subject of the day, and people have a great deal to say about it. A young man by the name of Patrick Henry is strongly opposed to this new tax imposed by the British, and he has said so in the House of Burgesses.

Williamsburg is the thriving capital of Virginia. Ships laden with silk, spices, wine, tea, and molasses sail up the James and York Rivers to deliver these goods to nearby ports. Some of the imports are legal, but some are not! Tobacco is Virginia's most valuable cash crop, and it can be used as currency.

Most of the people here are law-abiding citizens, but some are—how shall I put this?—unsavory characters. Convicted criminals from England are sent to work in the tobacco fields rather than take up space in British prisons. There are counterfeiters minting their own coins and imposters who are simply not who they say they are. Pirates, smugglers, and rogues mix with shopkeepers, merchants, and farmers.

Sadly, there are also many enslaved Black people who have been kidnapped in West and North African countries and brought here against their will. For the most part they work in the fields planting and harvesting tobacco, and making their enslavers rich. They are denied all freedoms, and they receive not a penny for the long hours, days, months, and years of hard work.

Williamsburg has laws in place, of course. If someone is found guilty of murder, piracy, treason, or burglary, they could face the noose! Other crimes are less obvious. Do not bake bad bread or make bad beer. Do not fail to attend church at least once a month. Be willing to devote some of your time to putting out fires or repairing the roads. Speaking of roads—keep them clean. Do not gossip, bicker, swear, commit slander, or exhibit lazy behavior in public. Do not fight unless it is a duel. Do not dance on Sunday. You are a child until you turn fourteen. After that, should you break the law, you will be tried as an adult.

Constables and watchmen maintain law and order and apprehend criminals, often with the aid of townsfolk. Men have more legal rights than women, and only free white men who own land and attend church are allowed to vote.

As you take in the sights and sounds, know that five laws are being willfully abandoned. Which ones might they be?

I MUST PURCHASE NEW SMELLING SALTS.
DISGUSTING!
YOU ARE LATE!
ANNA NO LONGER GOES TO CHURCH.
MY WORD!
I WILL EAT AT THE TAVERN.
GIDDY UP, TILDA!
HIS SERMON WAS RATHER CONFUSING.

KINGS ARMS
RUM
FINEST RUM IN THE COLONY!
FRESH AND TASTY!
YOU BE QUIET!
WHY DON'T YOU BE QUIET?!
WHY, THANK YOU!
SOON I WILL BE RICH!

Law & Order in Colonial Virginia

Virginia is a British colony, so its laws are based on English common law. There are also new laws that cover public behavior, attending church, flirting, speaking disrespectfully of government, and public hygiene. Separate from these laws is the brutal and racist slave code, which outlines the treatment of enslaved Black people.

Often a person's social status will determine how severe a punishment is. The higher one's social class, the less painful the punishment. More often than not, enslaved people receive the harshest physical punishments.

Generally speaking, punishment is swift for people who break the law. Those who commit petty crimes typically face public humiliation. Jail is mostly reserved for those people unable to pay a fine or a tax. Offenses such as public drunkenness, brawling, hog theft, and blasphemy are not tolerated. For these crimes, people are fined and sometimes tied to a post and whipped. Of course, for the *most* serious crimes, the convicted criminal will be hanged.

There is one possible way to escape the death penalty. It is called benefit of clergy. If a person can read or recite a biblical passage, they may be spared the noose and instead be forced to labor for several years.

Those who are repeatedly drunk and disorderly are branded with a *D*. Thieves are branded with a *T* and often whipped or put in a pillory, with an ear or possibly two nailed to the frame. If a thief keeps stealing, they will face the death penalty. People who bicker in public may be tied to a ducking chair and dunked in a river or lake.

For those who gossip, there is the gossip's bridle. A heavy iron helmet is placed over the gossiper's head, and a flat piece of iron is forced into the mouth to hold the tongue in place.

What eye-watering reprimands await those who broke the law here in Williamsburg?

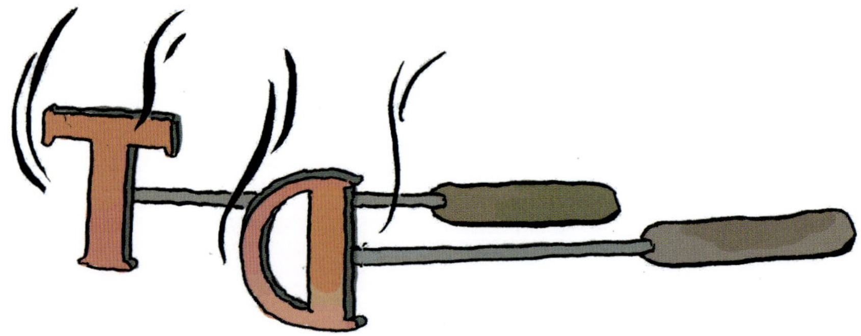

Crimes & Punishments

Crime 1
Gossip & Slander

Martha has falsely accused Anna of not attending church. She must now wear the painful and humiliating gossip's bridle for two days.

Crime 2
Smuggling

Charles is guilty of illegally bringing rum into Virginia. Some judges have turned a blind eye toward smuggling because they believe in free trade, not unfair British taxes. Nevertheless, Charles will be fined five pounds.

Crime 3
Counterfeiting

James has been printing forged paper currency, a most serious offense. As this is his first crime, he won't face the noose. Instead, he will be indentured for seven years of hard labor.

Crime 4
Bickering in Public

Mr. and Mrs. Witherspoon have been bickering *again* in the street. Now they must face the ducking chair. They will be tied back to back and dunked in the river several times.

Crime 5
Breaking Public Hygiene Laws

Katherine has been warned about throwing dirty, smelly water into the street. Now she and her husband will be fined, and Katherine may end up in the pillory!

II. Crime Location: Sacramento, California, 1851 CE

Hold on to your hat, for you now find yourself on a warm summer's evening in the rapidly expanding town of Sacramento, California, in the year 1851 CE. People from just about everywhere are flocking here hoping to strike it rich. The desire for gold is riling folks up, so be careful!

Yes, those were indeed gunshots you just heard. Stay calm and don't run. Most folks here carry firearms, and people are used to the sound of gunfire. I would casually walk in the other direction if I were you. Feel free to spit nonchalantly!

It all began in 1848, about two years before California joined the Union. James Marshall found small flakes of gold at Sutter's Sawmill in Coloma, thirty-six miles northeast of Sacramento. Marshall tried to keep his discovery a secret, but word got out. The year 1849 saw thousands of people hopping onto ships and wagons bound for California, all dreaming of becoming rich. This wave of immigration was made up of young American men and women, including free African Americans, as well as people from Mexico, Europe, and China.

Before the influx, Native peoples such as the Nisenan, Kumeyaay, and Miwok tribes lived on this land and cared for it. Now some of them have been pushed aside or seen the natural resources on their land destroyed. Others have bravely resisted by attempting to defend their land with force. All have seen their numbers rapidly decline due to diseases brought by the newcomers.

The desire for wealth is driving all this. Some miners are so consumed by greed that they are said to have "gold fever." Some clever folks have figured out there's even more money to be made selling supplies to miners. Shovels, picks, food, and clothing are selling like hotcakes.

Stand back! It looks like those two boys on horseback are in a hurry to leave town! The notion of taking the law into one's own hands is widely practiced here, which is why the man in the wide-brimmed hat is shooting at the boys. The sheriff doesn't complain about vigilantes much, as he has his hands full. For better or worse, it's often everyday folk who help keep things in check around here. You see, what was once a fairly law-abiding place is no longer.

There are *all* kinds of folks living side by side here, including bandits and fraudsters. There are also many ways in which you can be cheated and generally bamboozled. If someone offers to make you rich overnight or miraculously cure an illness, SAY NO! And do not drink anything referred to as "fire water."

Although laws in Sacramento are difficult to enforce, they *do* exist. It is against the law to rob a bank or stagecoach, or shoot or swindle someone—though these crimes happen fairly frequently. Being a vagrant is a crime, as is causing a public disturbance. However, should you wish to become a prizefighter, a professional gambler, or even an alchemist who mixes healing concoctions, go right ahead!

And now for your last challenge. On this particular evening, can you detect the four crimes being committed in the Wild West town of Sacramento?

BANK
9
SALOON
6
OH NO! NOT AGAIN!
HURRY!
OOOMPH!
LAND'S SAKE!
ARRRGH!
MY FAMILY WILL ARRIVE TOMORROW!

NEWS
WELL, LOOK WHO JUST RODE INTO TOWN!
THIS IS MY KIND OF PLACE!
MOVE ALONG—NOW!
18
GENERAL
HARDWARE
I CAN REPAIR YOUR COAT FOR A SMALL FEE.
QUICK! TAKE THIS!
YOU HAVE A DEAL!
THE SOLUTION TO ALL YOUR TROUBLES IS IN THIS BOTTLE!

Law & Order During the California Gold Rush

California has recently become a state, so American laws now apply in Sacramento. If the laws are broken, the punishments should apply too. But this is not always the case, largely because it is difficult to enforce the law in such a rapidly expanding town. Sacramento has an inadequate jail, few judges, and only one sheriff. Often criminals are dealt with in a haphazard way, and punishments are carried out by members of the community.

Petty criminals, such as folks who pick pockets, get drunk and cause a public disturbance, or cheat their customers, face being fined, horsewhipped, dunked in a horse trough, or run out of town. Vagrancy is a crime, but that law is too often used against the Native people of this area. Murder or bank robbery will get a person hanged.

Grievances are often settled before the law can step in. Shoot-outs are fairly common, even though they are technically against the law. The sheriff sometimes has no choice but to look the other way.

There are few laws that protect the rights of Native peoples. And the laws that do exist are often ignored. In truth, there is no real justice for them.

Crimes committed in the gold mining camps are dealt with there. Some of the camps are wild places. Drunkenness, cursing, gambling, and even brawling are everyday occurrences. But there are rules. Stealing from a fellow miner will get the thief in a lot of trouble. For a small theft, the thief will be banished or lashed, and possibly branded. For those who steal valuable items, the outcome is bleak: The thief will be hanged or shot.

What punishments await the criminals in this rough and ready town?

Crimes & Punishments

Crime 1
Vagrancy

Victor is a poet—a man of words. However, Victor has fallen on hard times and has nowhere to live. Vagrants are thought to be troublemakers or even criminals. Victor will be driven out of town in a wagon, left in a remote place, and told to keep on walking.

Crime 2
Creating a Public Disturbance

Chris and Jacob fought over a card game. Both men will be dunked in a river. Then after a few swift kicks to their posteriors, they will be sent on their way.

Crime 3
Breaking into a Store & Stealing

Mining supplies are in high demand. Max and Andrew planned to steal mining equipment and sell it to new arrivals. As the value of the equipment is considered high, they will be hanged.

Crime 4
Bank Robbery

Siblings Jack and Avery have just become bank robbers. Jack wasted all the family's money searching for gold—and then tried to fix things by robbing a bank. For this serious crime, Jack will face the noose, while Avery will be imprisoned for several years. Good behavior could win her an early release.

Debriefing

Welcome back, intrepid time-traveling sleuth! I do hope your experiences were not too discomforting. As you have discovered, societies over time and across many continents have been faced with the difficult challenges of managing large populations, determining what rules seem reasonable, and deciding what to do when people don't follow those rules. As you have also discovered, what is considered an illegal act can vary according to the society and the period in time. The punishments vary considerably too!

As far back as we can tell, there have been criminals as well as punishments. Many people throughout history have failed to follow rules or legal expectations—for a whole range of reasons.

Let's face it, humans aren't perfect, and legal systems aren't perfect either. Understanding how an ancient desert kingdom, a crowded medieval city, and a newly established Gold Rush town dealt with similar challenges is, at the very least, eye-opening. Such knowledge allows us to trace the human experience through time and place. No doubt people in the future will reflect upon us—and how we manage such challenges. I can't help but wonder what conclusions they will draw.

And now I bid you farewell, dear reader. May we meet again in some other time and place. Until then, continue to seek adventures, ask questions, and stay out of trouble!

Until we meet again,
The Author

Glossary

accusation: A claim that someone has done something wrong or unlawful.

administrator: A person who manages or organizes a designated place.

apprehend: To catch, seize, or arrest a person.

artisan: A skilled artist or worker.

assault: A physical attack.

banishment: A punishment that forces someone to leave a place and not return for a period of time—or ever.

bicker: To argue about silly things.

Black Death: An outbreak of bubonic plague that killed millions of people in Europe in the 1300s.

blasphemy: Language that is offensive to certain religious beliefs.

bushido: A code of honor created by Japanese samurai.

chivalry: The customs or ways of knighthood.

citizen: A person who belongs to a country, kingdom, or empire.

city-state: A city that has independent control over its people, economy, political structure, and defense.

class: A division within a society that is based on social and economic levels.

consul: The most important official in the Roman Republic.

counterfeit: To create an imitation of something, often money, in order to deceive.

court of law: A place where cases are heard, often by a judge or judges, and a decision is determined.

cubit: An ancient unit of length that measured approximately 18 inches (about 46 centimeters).

curfew: An order that people must stay home between certain hours.

custom: A traditional way of acting or doing something.

death penalty: Death as a form of punishment.

debt: The state of owing money. A debtor is a person who owes money.

dictator: A ruler who has full control.

disenfranchise: To take away a person's rights or privileges.

divine right: The belief that a ruler's power comes from God.

ducking chair: A chair attached to a long pole that can be lowered into water.

duel: A contest between two people with weapons in order to settle a disagreement.

eavesdrop: To listen to a private conversation.

empire: A large territory, or many territories, controlled by a single ruler, who is sometimes called an emperor or empress.

equestrian class: A fighting and landowning class in ancient Rome, below the patrician and senatorial classes but above commoners.

evidence: Information that helps prove or disprove an accusation. False evidence is made up to mislead.

feudal lord: A nobleman who bestows land on people, or allows people to use his land, in exchange for their service.

forgery: The act of creating something false, such as a document or signature.

fraud: Deceit or trickery.

governor: The leader of a colony, state, or province.

hard labor: Forced physical work.

imposter: A person who pretends to be someone else.

incantation: Words spoken or sung as part of a ritual.

Islamic law: A code of law based on the Quran, the sacred text of Islam.

Glossary

juror: A person who considers the evidence and makes a decision in a trial. A group of jurors is called a jury.

justice: A determination or decision made in relation to the established laws of a society.

knight: A mounted soldier who serves a lord or a king.

leprosy: A contagious bacterial disease, also known as Hansen's disease.

lord: A person with power and authority in society.

magistrate: A person who has the ability to make legal decisions.

merchant: A buyer and seller of goods.

Middle Ages: The period in European history that followed the fall of the Roman Empire, from about 500 CE to the 1400s or 1500s. Also called the medieval period.

mosque: A place of worship or prayer for Muslims.

noble: A person belonging to a very high social class.

oath: A promise. A person who is "under oath" in court has promised to tell the truth.

patrician: A member of ancient Rome's highest social class; a wealthy landowner in ancient Rome.

petty crime: A minor offense.

pharaoh: A ruler in ancient Egypt.

philosophy: The study of life's key questions.

pictogram: A graphic symbol that has meaning.

pilgrimage: A journey made by a pilgrim, a religious person who travels to a holy place.

pillory: A structure with holes designed to hold a person's head and hands as a form of punishment.

plebeian: A common person in ancient Rome.

politics: Activities and ideas that influence government actions.

pope: The head of the Roman Catholic Church.

province: An area or region of a country or kingdom.

rebellion: An act of resistance against those in authority.

samurai: A Japanese warrior who has promised loyalty and service to a lord.

scribe: A person whose job is to record information.

senator: A member of the Senate, the lawmaking body in ancient Rome.

shogun: A ruling military chief in feudal Japan.

slander: A false statement spoken about a person.

smuggler: A person who illegally moves goods, sometimes stolen, in and out of a place.

social order: The rank and order of people within a society, often based on family and wealth.

Stamp Act: A tax imposed on paper products in the American colonies by the British.

Tang Code: A Chinese penal code that outlined or explained laws in relation to crimes.

tax: Money that people must pay to the government.

trade: The buying and selling of goods.

treason: The crime of betraying one's country or its leader.

vagrant: A person without a permanent home.

verdict: A decision that is made in a court of law.

vigilante: A person with no authority who attempts to enforce the law and punish perceived criminals.

virtuous: To act in a moral manner, as defined by the principles of the time.

vizier: A high-level official who has the ability to make decisions.

Selected Bibliography

Arnaoutoglou, Ilias. *Ancient Greek Laws: A Sourcebook.* Routledge, 1998.

Bauman, Richard A. *Crime and Punishment in Ancient Rome.* Routledge, 1996.

BBC. "Tokugawa Ieyasu (1542–1616)." https://www.bbc.co.uk/history/historic_figures/ieyasu_tokugawa.shtml.

Britannica. "Greek Law." Updated September 6, 2011. https://www.britannica.com/topic/Greek-law.

Britannica. "Middle Ages." Updated October 2, 2025. https://www.britannica.com/event/Middle-Ages.

Britannica. "Solon's Laws." Updated March 31, 2020. https://www.britannica.com/topic/Solons-laws.

Cohen, Daniel A. *Pillars of Salt, Monuments of Grace: New England Crime Literature and the Origins of American Popular Culture, 1674–1860*. University of Massachusetts Press, 2006.

Colonial Williamsburg. "Discover the People & Places That Shaped America." https://www.colonialwilliamsburg.org/discover/.

Dash, Mike. "The Demonization of Empress Wu." *Smithsonian Magazine*. August 10, 2012. http://www.smithsonianmag.com/history/the-demonization-of-empress-wu-20743091/.

Frye, R. N., Soden, W. T. V., and Edzard, D. O. "History of Mesopotamia." *Britannica*. Updated October 27, 2025. https://www.britannica.com/place/Mesopotamia-historical-region-Asia.

Graft-Johnson, J. C. D. "Mūsā I of Mali." *Britannica*. Updated September 12, 2025. https://www.britannica.com/biography/Musa-I-of-Mali.

Grummond, N. T. D., et al. "Ancient Rome." *Britannica*. Updated October 11, 2025. https://www.britannica.com/place/ancient-Rome.

History.com. "San Francisco." Updated May 28, 2025. https://www.history.com/topics/us-states/san-francisco.

Jarus, Owen. "Tenochtitlán: History of Aztec Capital." Live Science. Updated August 17, 2022. https://www.livescience.com/34660-tenochtitlan.html.

Krasner, Barbara. *Mansa Musa: The Most Famous African Traveler to Mecca*. Rosen Young Adult, 2016.

Medieval Europe. Core Knowledge Foundation, 2017.

Mexicolore. "Aztecs." https://www.mexicolore.co.uk/aztecs/.

PBS. "The Roman Empire in the First Century." https://www.pbs.org/empires/romans/empire/order.html.

Teon, Aris. "China's Legal System and the 'Ten Abominations.'" Greater China Journal. May 11, 2016. https://china-journal.org/2016/05/11/china-legal-system-ten-abominations/.

Tyldesley, Joyce. *Judgement of the Pharaoh: Crime and Punishment in Ancient Egypt*. Orion Publishing, 2000.

Vaver, Anthony. *Bound with an Iron Chain: The Untold Story of How the British Transported 50,000 Convicts to Colonial America*. Pickpocket Publishing, 2011.

Wilson, Elizabeth B. "The Queen Who Would Be King." *Smithsonian Magazine*. September 2006. https://www.smithsonianmag.com/history/the-queen-who-would-be-king-130328511/.

Zhangsun Wuji. "Selections from the Great Tang Code: Article 6, 'The Ten Abominations.'" Asia for Educators. http://afe.easia.columbia.edu/ps/cup/zhangsun_wuji_great_tang_code.pdf.

Index

To Anna and Chris and to my Semester at Sea shipmates who helped shape the idea for this book—R. M.

To my wife, Carolina, for sharing the dream and constantly reminding me that drawing pictures isn't just what I do, but a lifestyle we have embraced as a family—D. O.

Very special thanks to Dr. Kristen McCleary, professor of history at James Madison University, and Dr. Mark G. Spencer, professor of history at Brock University, for sharing their invaluable expertise and advice.

Charlesbridge • 9 Galen Street, Watertown, MA 02472 • www.charlesbridge.com

Library of Congress Cataloging-in-Publication Data
Names: McCormick, Rosie author | Otero, Diegofer illustrator
Title: Crimes through time: mischief, missteps & dastardly deeds / Rosie McCormick; illustrated by Diegofer Otero.
Description: Watertown, MA: Charlesbridge, [2026] | Includes bibliographical references and index. | Audience: Ages 9–12 | Audience: Grades 4–6 | Summary: "A cheeky narrator challenges readers to spot the crimes in this interactive time-traveling adventure that introduces the laws of the land from Ancient Egypt to the California Gold Rush."—Provided by publisher.
Identifiers: LCCN 2025014678 (print) | LCCN 2025014679 (ebook) | ISBN 9781580898461 hardcover | ISBN 9781632897053 ebook
Subjects: LCSH: Crime—History—Juvenile literature | Criminal law—History—Juvenile literature | LCGFT: Literature
Classification: LCC HV6027.M334 2026 (print) | LCC HV6027 (ebook) | DDC 364—dc23/eng/20250923
LC record available at https://lccn.loc.gov/2025014678
LC ebook record available at https://lccn.loc.gov/2025014679

Printed in China • OPIC
The authorized representative in the EU for product safety and compliance is eucomply OÜ, Pärnu mnt 139b-14, 11317 Tallinn, Estonia, hello@eucompliancepartner.com, +33757690241
(hc) 10 9 8 7 6 5 4 3 2 1

Illustrations done in pen and ink and colored digitally
Text type set in Museo Slab
Edited by Alyssa Mito Pusey
Designed by Diane Earley
Production supervised by Nicole Turner